Copyright 2020 - by Beth Costanzo

www.adventuresofscubajack.com

In our exploration of some of our oceans' most fascinating creatures, we have finally arrived on one of the coolest looking fish. In fact, if you have seen the movie Finding Nemo, you will know what I'm talking about: **The Clownfish**.

www.adventuresofscubajack.com

The **clownfish** is a beautiful fish. Depending on the particular species, you can find **clownfish** in colors like yellow, orange, or a blackish or reddish color. Along with these distinctive colors, **clownfish** show many white patches or bars.

This orange color and white bar, for instance, is what Nemo and Marlin look like in *Finding Nemo*. Their distinctive colors make **clownfish** some of the most recognizable and stunning fish in our waters.

www.adventuresofscubajack.com

Clownfish, compared to other fish in our oceans, are pretty small. The largest **clownfish** can reach about 6.7 inches while the smallest is about 2.8 to 3.1 inches long. Overall, **clownfish** need to be careful when swimming because larger predators can eat them.

There are many different species of **clownfish**. In fact, there are 30 of them. These 30 species of **clownfish** live in several different habits. Most notably, they are found in the warmer waters of the Indian and Pacific Oceans. If you are on vacation in Japan, Southeast Asia, Indonesia, or Australia, you may be able to spot a **clownfish** in the wild. Having said this, **clownfish** often live at the bottom of shallow seas, meaning that you may need to snorkel or scuba dive to see them. These fish live in sheltered reefs or shallow lagoons and near things called sea anemones. These sea anemones, among other things, can help protect **clownfish** from predators.

www.adventuresofscubajack.com

Clownfish are omnivores. This means that they eat both fish and plants. Some of their favorite foods include small zooplankton along with algae. Along with this food, **clownfish** may also eat on some of the undigested food found on anemones.

As far as predators, **clownfish** may be eaten by larger fish, sharks, and eels. But putting aside those fish, one of the greatest threats to **clownfish** is humans. Humans don't eat **clownfish**, but rather catch them and put them in tanks or aquariums.

www.adventuresofscubajack.com

Because of this, **clownfish** have a very unique relationship with sea anemones. The sea anemone helps protect the **clownfish** from predators and provide scraps of food that the **clownfish** can enjoy. It can also serve as a nest site for the **clownfish**.

As for the **clownfish**, it gives back to the sea anemone in a number of ways. First, the **clownfish** can defend the sea anemone from different types of predators and parasites. The **clownfish**'s frequent swimming around the sea anemone can create greater water circulation. The nitrogen that leaves the **clownfish**'s body can even increase the number of algae in the sea anemone, which can help the anemone in tissue growth and tissue regeneration.

www.adventuresofscubajack.com

As you can see, the **clownfish** and sea anemone need each other. They provide lots of help to each other and can make each other safer and healthier. So if you see a **clownfish** in the wild, don't be surprised if you see a sea anemone nearby.

One of the most fascinating things about **clownfish** is the way that they have babies and get older. In terms of babies, **clownfish** lay their eggs on a flat surface that is close to their sea anemone. Depending on the specific species, some **clownfish** can lay hundreds or thousands of eggs at a time. The male parent of the eggs guards the eggs until they hatch (which is often two hours after sunset).

www.adventuresofscubajack.com

www.adventuresofscubajack.com

Finally, one of the coolest things about **clownfish** is the way that they communicate. **Clownfish** talk to each other by making popping and clicking noises. Even though we may not be able to hear them while we're swimming, they are speaking to each other. One of the main reasons is that they are trying to prevent fights. It helps keep the group in line so that conflict does not break out.

Clownfish Activities

www.adventuresofscubajack.com

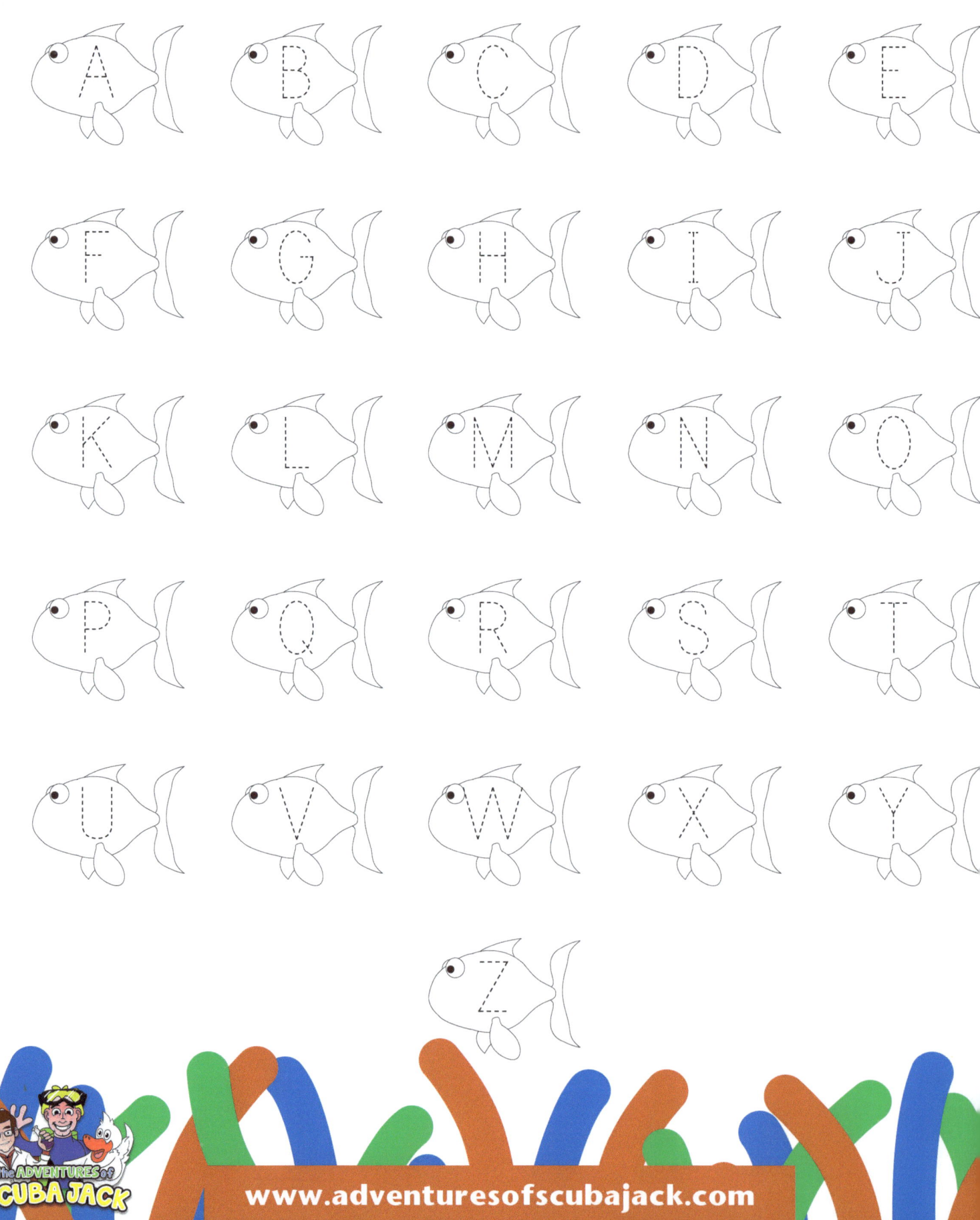

TRACING

Trace the word below then write it.

Clownfish

COUNTING

Count the Clownfish then circle the correct answer.

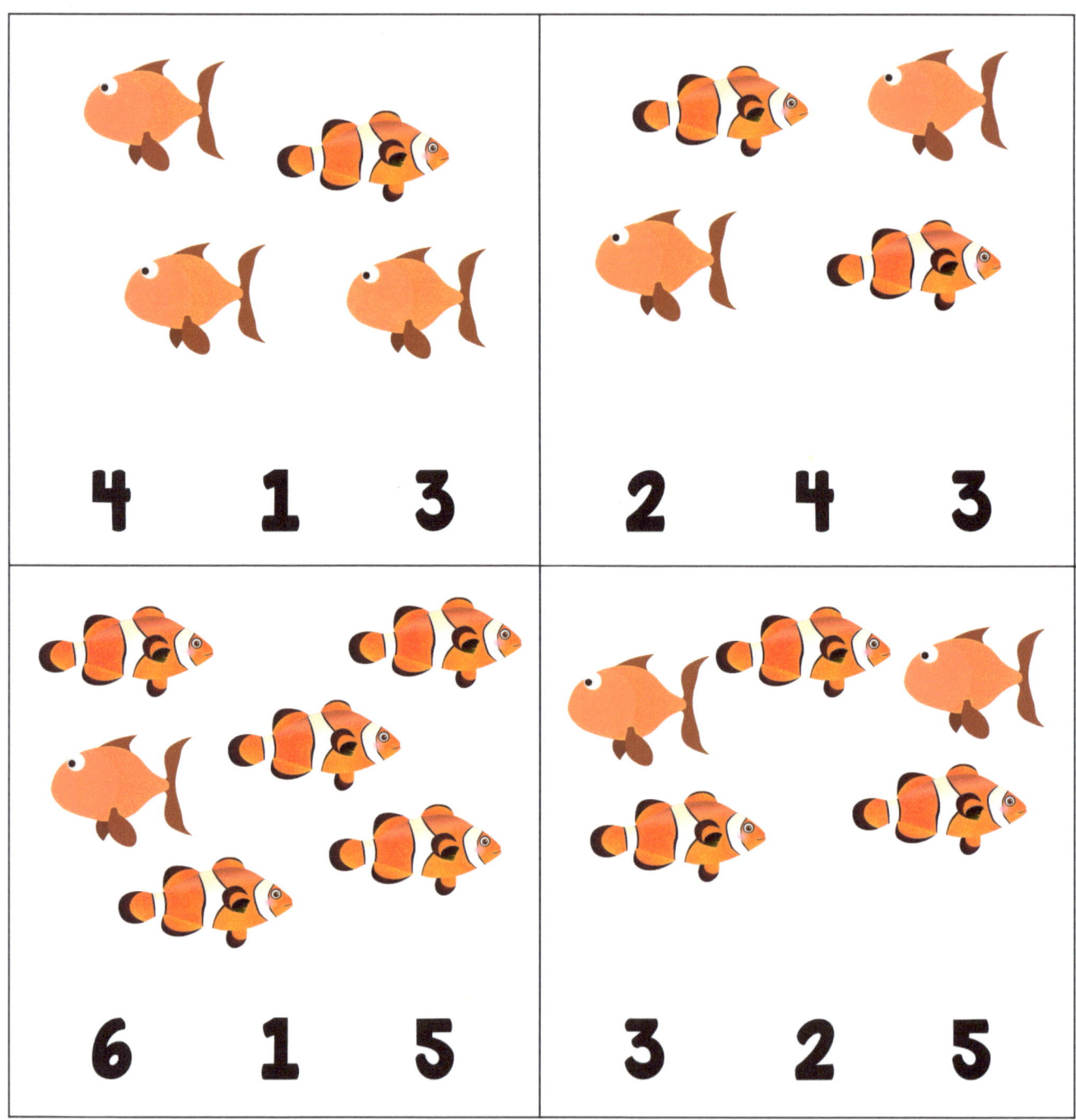

COUNTING

Count the Clownfish then put the anwer in the boxes.

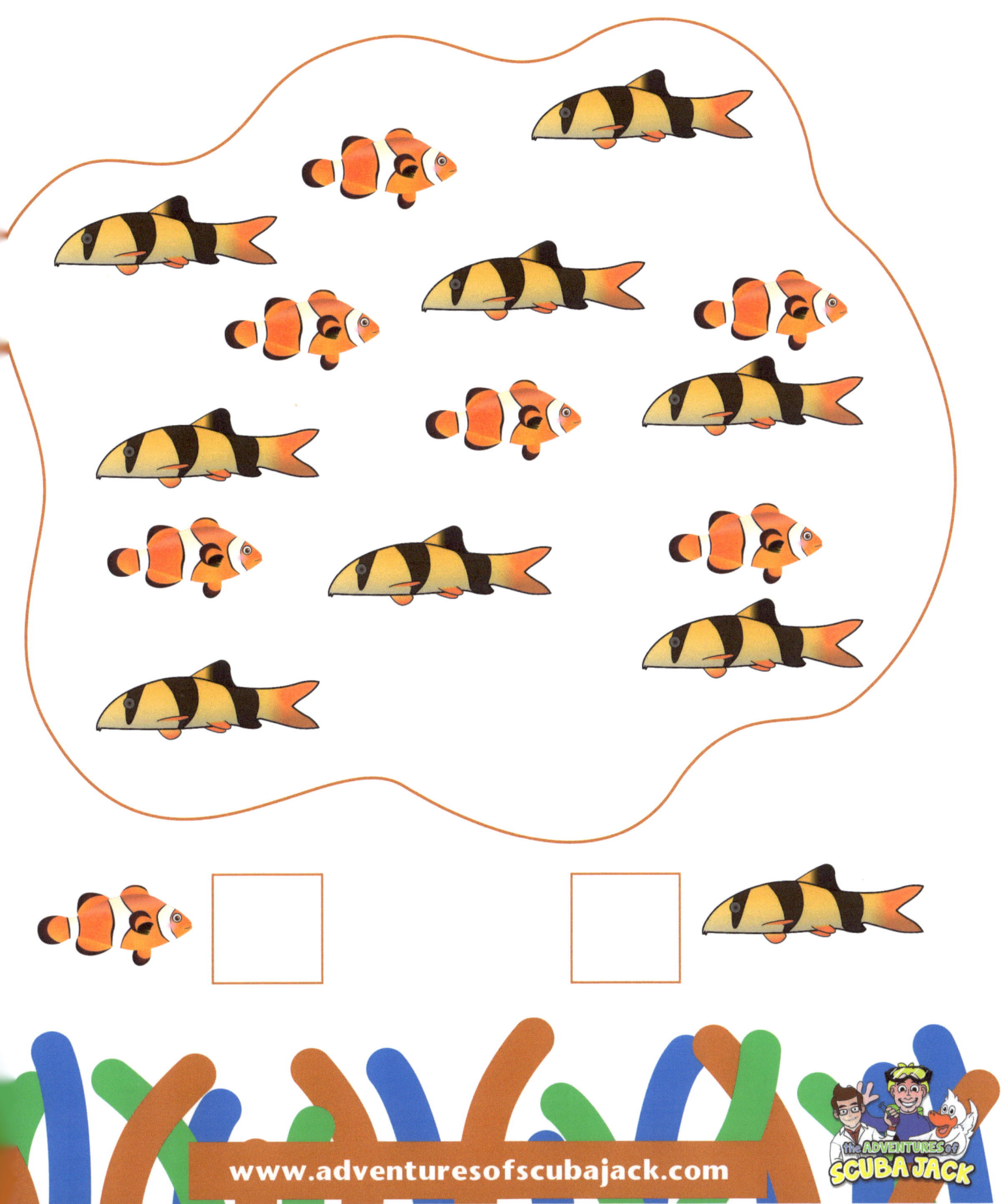

COLORING
Color the drawing below.

COLORING
Color the drawing below.

www.adventuresofscubajack.com

Visit us at
www.adventuresofscubajack.com

Watch Our Amazing Clownfish Video.
Try Your Expertise With Our Amazing Clownfish Quiz!

www.ingramcontent.com/pod-product-compliance
Lightning Source LLC
Chambersburg PA
CBHW041438010526
44118CB00002B/119